The Smartest Woman I Know

Also by ILENE BECKERMAN

Love, Loss, and What I Wore

What We Do for Love

Mother of the Bride:
The Dream, the Reality, the Search for a Perfect Dress

Makeovers at the Beauty Counter of Happiness

THE
SMARTEST
WOMAN
I KNOW

by Ilene Beckerman

ALGONQUIN BOOKS OF CHAPEL HILL 2011

Published by
Algonquin Books of Chapel Hill
Post Office Box 2225
Chapel Hill, North Carolina 27515-2225

a division of Workman Publishing
225 Varick Street
New York, New York 10014

Printed in Mexico.
Published simultaneously in Canada by Thomas Allen & Son Limited.
Design by Jacky Woolsey.

Library of Congress Cataloging-in-Publication Data
Beckerman, Ilene, [date]
The smartest woman I know / Ilene Beckerman. —1st ed.
p. cm.
ISBN 978-1-56512-537-7
1. Beckerman, Ilene, [date]. 2. Goldberg, Ettie. 3. Grandmothers—United
States—Biography. 4. Jewish women—United States—Biography. I. Title.
CT275.B5476A3 2011
973.931092—dc23
[B]
2011020092

10 9 8 7 6 5 4 3 2 1
First Edition

The Smartest Woman I Know

WHOEVER SAID there's nobody as smart as an old woman must have known my grandmother, Ettie. If she had been born in the late twentieth century instead of the late nineteenth century, she probably would have been the superstar of advice bloggers.

The older I get, the more often I think about Ettie and the more her words come back to me. Sometimes you don't know how much you love somebody until that somebody's gone.

First, a Little Background

IF THE GOLDBERGS HADN'T left Grodno in Russia in the late nineteenth century . . .

If they hadn't ended up in New Orleans and started a business tanning hides for drum heads . . .

If Lillie Young, my grandmother Ettie, then a young girl, hadn't left the Big Apple in 1901 and traveled to the Big Easy to visit her relatives . . .

If she hadn't met her distant cousin Harry Goldberg in New Orleans on October 1, 1901 . . .

If Harry Goldberg hadn't married her on October 26, 1901, twenty-six days after they met . . .

If Harry's father hadn't had such a fierce temper, Harry might not have taken his bride and headed for New York . . .

If Harry and his bride hadn't settled on the Lower East

From left: Harry Goldberg, Ettie, and the New Orleans relatives

Side, both working seventeen hours a day in a candy store and saving every penny . . .

If they hadn't saved enough pennies to buy a building to open their own candy store . . .

If it weren't 1929 and the Depression hadn't come at the same time that Harry was about to close on the building . . .

If the bank that Harry had asked for a loan hadn't reneged because of the Depression . . .

If when Harry, hat in hand, went to his rich relative,

Mr. Gertz, to borrow money and Mr. Gertz hadn't said, "You should have come yesterday . . ."

If when Harry, again with hat in hand, hadn't gone to the Empire Trust Company on Madison Avenue and 56th Street near the building Harry wanted to buy . . .

If Mr. Smith, the loan officer, hadn't believed in Harry and agreed to lend him the money he needed . . .

Then there never would have been a candy store called Goldberg's in the farmland of upper Manhattan . . .

And the store wouldn't have changed its name to Madison Stationers when the farmland turned into the ritzy neighborhood of the Upper East Side.

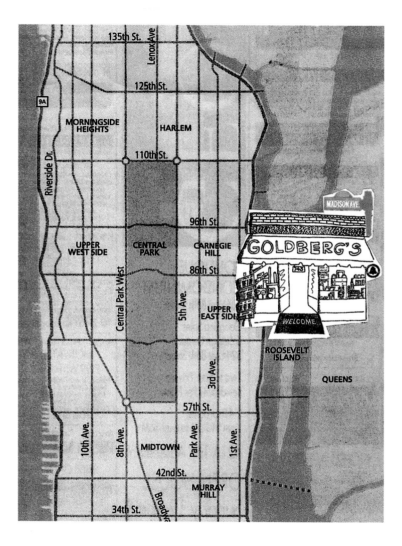

THE STORY BEGINS

UNLIKE THE PIONEERS WHO went west, Ettie
(no one remembers why Lillie acquired that nickname) and
Mr. Goldberg (no one remembers when Harry decided that he
should only be referred to as Mr. Goldberg) were pioneers who
went north.

They left the safety and familiarity of the Lower East
Side, where a sour pickle, a bialy, or a two-cents plain were
only a block away, and moved to Madison Avenue between
64th and 65th streets. After years of living on Madison
Avenue, they became gentrified on the outside but never
in their hearts. Instead of a jelly donut from a pushcart on
Second Avenue, Mr. Goldberg would buy a Linzer tart from

Duvanoy's, the French bakery on
Madison and 65th Street.

Instead of hanging the wash on
a clothesline from the kitchen window,
Ettie sent the wash to the Chinese
laundry on Lexington Avenue. But
every bone in their body was Jewish,
and despite living in this wonderful
land of opportunity, they were always
on guard. The next Hitler or Stalin
could be waiting around the corner on
64th Street.

THIS STORY IS MOSTLY about Ettie, all 4'10" of her.
She was one of the smartest women I ever knew, even though
she never made it past the third grade.

Also in the story are:

Mr. Goldberg, who at four o'clock every afternoon, left
the store and went upstairs where he and Ettie lived, to take a
nap in his blue easy chair.

And God, to whom Ettie spoke several times a day . . .

You got a minute, God? I'm not really complaining but it says in the Talmud that a man has 613 mitzvahs to do but a woman only has 3. So how come I am busy from the minute I wake up in the morning until I go to bed at night, and Mr. Goldberg, who has 613 mitzvahs to do, has enough time to go upstairs at four o'clock every afternoon and take a nap?

Two other characters in the story are:

Tootsie, my sister, older than me and much prettier, who I occasionally hated . . .

and Gingy, me.

My sister and I went to live with Ettie and Mr. Goldberg in 1947, when I was twelve years old and my sister was seventeen. The reason we went to live with them is a story for another day.

A few years earlier in Atlantic City

The first year we lived there, Ettie cried a lot. Sometimes because she was peeling an onion. Sometimes because President Roosevelt had died. Sometimes because of things I was too young to understand at the time.

I remember Tootsie going out on a first date with a boy from Westchester that year. She thought he had money. He thought she had money. Both were wrong.

I remember hiding a paperback copy of *Forever Amber*, the hottest, bawdiest book of the time in an *Adventures of Superman* comic book.

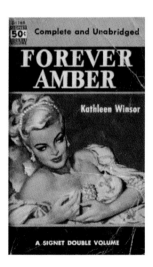

"'I'm sorry,' he said softly. 'I didn't expect to find you a virgin.'"

Forever Amber? In my house? The Talmud's not good enough for her?

Tootsie lived with Ettie and Mr. Goldberg for one year, until she got married at eighteen. I lived with Ettie and Mr. Goldberg for six years, until I went to college.

Some of the things I remember about those six years might not really have happened. I might have mixed up my memories with my sister's memories or with movies I saw. Sort of like the Kurosawa movie *Rashomon*. In that movie, many witnesses to the same event describe in detail what they saw. Each recollection is different.

No!   **Yes!**

Rashomon

If there was only one way of looking at something, God wouldn't have given you two eyes.

To me, everything I'm going to tell you really happened. Like the time I was fifteen and bought a black dress for a New Year's Eve party and Ettie said to me, "You're wearing black? You're going to a funeral?"

Maybe what happened in those small moments shaped my life more than I realized. Maybe we are the memories we hold on to. Things that happened a long time ago seem to have happened yesterday. Even now, sixty years later, when I wear a black dress, I remember Ettie's words.

DURING THE YEARS I lived with Ettie and Mr. Goldberg, the world changed a lot. World War II had ended, Jackie Robinson broke the color barrier in baseball, Israel became a state, long-playing vinyl phonograph records and the Diners Club credit card were introduced, Senator Joseph McCarthy conducted a "witch hunt," the Rosenbergs were executed, 50 percent of Americans owned television sets, and the Korean War ended.

But during that time, life didn't change very much for Ettie. After raising three children while working in the store seven days a week, she found herself, at the age of sixty-five, raising two grandchildren while working in the store seven days a week.

Just about all day, everyday, Ettie would either be standing by the cash register, waiting on a customer, or sitting on a folding chair in the back of Goldberg's candy and stationery store holding court and schmoozing with the customers.

The Store

ANYBODY WHO WAS ANYBODY in the neighborhood—the *machers,* the mavens, the *meshuggeners*—came in to Goldberg's. Most of them weren't Jewish.

Loyal customers like Mr. Arnold, who never went out without his boater straw hat, spats, walking cane, and the young man by his side he called darling.

Mr. Goldberg didn't wait on them. Ettie went out of her way to be nice to them.

You understand about boyfriends of boys, God? I don't. But if I had to choose between a somebody who fights with somebody and a somebody who wants to make believe that a boy is his girlfriend, it should be my business? If it were up to me, everybody should mind their own business.

Mrs. Vanderhaven was also a regular customer. Her elbow-length gloves always matched the silk flowers on the wide-brimmed picture hats she always wore.

Ettie said she kept the tags on her dresses tucked in the sleeves so she could return them to Russeks of Fifth Avenue after she'd worn them a few times.

Every Friday, Mrs. Vanderhaven would buy two Will & Baumer ten-inch ivory candles for her dining room table. The first of every month, she'd come in and spend an hour standing at the magazine rack looking through *Vogue* and *Harper's Bazaar.*

"Madam," I once heard Mr. Goldberg say, "this is a store. We sell things. If you're not buying, it would be my honor to escort you to the public library on 58th Street."

Mrs. Vanderhaven

SARA DELANO ROOSEVELT, FDR'S mother, lived in a brownstone at 47 East 65th Street, around the corner from the store. Every once in a while 5'10" Sara, who ruled over her son Franklin and her daughter-in-law Eleanor, would come into the store and visit with 4'10" Ettie.

What did they have in common? They were both mothers of sons, so they both worried.

Sara worried about her son Franklin's future because of his polio. Ettie worried about her son Larry's future because of the draft.

"Don't worry," Ettie told Mrs. Roosevelt, "your son's got a good head on his shoulders. I bet someday he'll be president."

Ettie told that to every customer who had a son. "That's how you make a customer," she told me.

If a customer had a daughter, Ettie would say, "Don't worry. Your daughter's got a good head on her shoulders. I bet someday she grows up to marry the president."

Ettie   Sara

NOT EVERYBODY WHO CAME into the store was a "somebody."

Mrs. O'Reilly was an Irish governess who worked for a fancy lady on Park Avenue. Every other sentence out of her mouth was "Jesus, Mary, and Joseph."

Mrs. O'Reilly had come from Dublin when her hair was red and she still had freckles. Even after her hair turned gray and her freckles turned to liver spots, she spoke with a brogue.

She had three grown sons. One was a priest, one was a policeman, and one she never talked about.

What did Ettie and Mrs. O'Reilly have in common? They both worried.

Mrs. O'Reilly would come in with a cheery "And how are ya today, Mrs. Goldberg? Did ya have your good-morning tea?"

After Tootsie and me, what Ettie loved most was hot tea and lemon. It had to be Lipton tea. In a glass. She'd put a sugar cube in her mouth and sip the steaming tea through the sugar cube.

"Yes," Ettie would answer Mrs. O'Reilly. "Two glasses. Thank you for asking. But I know how much you like your Irish coffee."

Mrs. O'Reilly would say, "Indeed, I do. Indeed I do. But I have it at night after I take off my shoes and my girdle."

"*Kineahora*, Mrs. O'Reilly. You should only live and make a habit of it. You drink coffee. I drink tea. But otherwise we have so much in common."

"Because we both have three children?"

"No, I mean the Irish and Jews have so much in common."

"That's what's called malarkey, Mrs. Goldberg."

"You ever hear of corned beef? So, the Irish eat theirs with cabbage, we eat ours with a pickle."

"Mrs. Goldberg, are ya sure you never kissed the Blarney stone?"

"Kissed the Blarney stone? I never even kissed Mr. Goldberg."

ONE DAY MARLENE DIETRICH,
wrapped in furs, came into the store.
Immediately Mr. Goldberg hurried over
to wait on her.

"Madam," he said, "I recognize who
you are and I must tell you I have seen
every one of your movies and enjoyed
every one. You have brought great pleasure
into my life. Now, how may I be of service
to you?"

Dietrich smiled and asked for a pack of du Maurier
cigarettes.

"Madam, is there anything else I may do for you?"
Mr. Goldberg said.

"No, thank you very much," Dietrich answered, "you are so kind." She paid for the cigarettes and left the store.

Mr. Goldberg turned to Ettie and said, "You know who that was?"

"Of course," Ettie answered.

"What a thrill," Mr. Goldberg said. "To think that I just waited on Katharine Hepburn."

God, should I tell him?

Ettie knew about movie stars even though she rarely went to the movies. "Who needs the movies," she'd say. I should pay money to go to the movie to see craziness? I can just stay home and see craziness. A movie about what's happening downstairs and upstairs and out my window, no one would believe. Nobody could make a movie so good as what I see with my own eyes. I have enough worries without going to the movies. If I want a headache, God, I can just stay home."

NOT ONLY WASN'T ETTIE a movie fan, she also wasn't a sports fan. Every afternoon, the same men would come into the store, buy the evening newspaper, and the first thing they'd do is turn to the sports page.

"Sports?" she'd say. "Another waste of time!

"North Korea is making war on South Korea and all these dummkopfs want to know is who won a ball game? A man jumps up and tries to get the ball in a basket. He takes a stick and hits the ball so it should go in a hole in the ground. He takes a fatter stick and tries to hit the ball far away. He grabs a ball and runs with it and other men try to push him down.

On Delancey Street

"A woman would never be so meshugge. She sees a basket, she fills it with fruit. She sees a hole she fills it up. She sees a stick, she puts it someplace out of the way so nobody should trip or get poked in the eye. Somebody tries to push her down, she calls a policeman."

If Ettie had no one to talk to, she muttered to herself. "So much money for a man with a ball? Nobody even knows the value of money anymore," she'd mutter. "Nobody picks up a penny on the street. If Mr. Goldberg and me hadn't saved every penny, we'd still be living on Delancey Street. A penny earned is a penny you should save. A dollar is even better."

UPSTAIRS

WHEN THEY WEREN'T IN the store, Ettie and
Mr. Goldberg went to their apartment above the store, where
they ate, spoke Yiddish to each other (when they spoke to
each other), and slept until the next day's work.

Upstairs, Ettie had her radio.

"Thanks, God, for the radio," she would say. "I listen
every day. I don't have to buy a ticket. I don't have to go
someplace else. I don't have to stop what I'm doing to look.
I don't even have to sit down. I can be standing by the stove,
wearing my housedress, taking the fat off the chicken soup,
and the President of the United States can be talking to me."
Unlike other grandmothers in those days, Ettie actually spent
as little time in the kitchen as possible. The store was what
nurtured her.

When Ettie and Mr. Goldberg came
from Europe, many Jews went to bed hungry.
So for Ettie, the purpose of cooking was to
keep the stomach filled. Quantity was more
important than quality.

One day a customer asked Ettie what she was making
for dinner. "Food," she answered without hesitation.

"Eat," she would say
to me. "You shouldn't
go hungry. Nobody
should go hungry."

ETTIE COOKED BECAUSE she didn't believe in eating out. "A restaurant?" she'd say. "Why eat out when you have a kitchen?"

One day a customer told Ettie about a new restaurant that opened in the neighborhood. "That's wonderful," Ettie said. "I have to try it." After the customer left, I heard her muttering.

"I need to go to a fancy-schmancy place, God? How do I know what *khazeray* they're putting into anything? How do I know they wash their hands? In my house, you could eat off the bathroom floor. In some restaurants, you don't even want to go to the bathroom in their bathroom."

Ettie believed that food could solve all problems. "Feed your stomach, and the rest will take care of itself," she advised. "It's amazing what a few little prunes can do."

Her advice about mental problems? "What you put in your stomach will make you feel better than what a man with a beard and an accent tells you about your mother."

For depression, she suggested pot roast with potatoes and carrots. For anxiety, *kreplach* and chicken soup. Up one day, moody the next? Try blintzes with a little sugar or a little sour cream, depending.

What she couldn't understand was Chinese food. "Shrimp? Do the Chinese eat gefilte fish?"

Next to Tootsie and me and after hot tea and lemon, the thing Ettie loved most in the world was her own gefilte fish.

One day Mr. Goldberg brought home gefilte fish in a jar. "You crazy," Ettie said, "gefilte fish already made! In a jar. With a label. From Brooklyn!"

> **Let me tell you something, God.
> The world is going to hell.**

DESPITE HER OPINION about eating out, every once in a while Ettie would have an urge for a good sour pickle from Gus's on Essex Street, so she'd take Tootsie or me with her to the Lower East Side.

We'd taxi downtown. Ettie didn't ride on the subway. "When I'm dead, *kineahora*, they can put me underground. Before that, I'm not going." Ettie didn't take buses either. "They make so many stops, by the time I get where I'm going, I forgot why I'm going."

Sometimes we'd go for a pastrami sandwich at Katz's on Houston Street. Sometimes we'd get a potato or a kasha *knish* at Yona Schimmel's. We'd always bring home *rugelach* from Gertel's Kosher Bakery for Mr. Goldberg.

Our excursion lasted only until one of us needed a bathroom. Then we'd run for a taxi and ask the driver to drive fast.

LIVING WITH ETTIE and Mr. Goldberg meant living in a kosher house. I was always constipated.

"But why can't I mix meat and milk?" I asked Ettie a million times. "The cow does."

Monte

Ettie was always trying to fatten me up. All I ever wanted was a grilled cheese sandwich and a cherry Coke at Liggett's Drug Store on 65th and Madison, made by the boy behind the counter who looked like Montgomery Clift, if Montgomery Clift had acne.

ETTIE TRIED TO ADAPT to me and to modern times. She used paper plates.

"Thank you, God, for making such a miracle. Okay, so paper plates may not be as big a deal as penicillin, but can I use penicillin to put food on that's not kosher? And for my grandchildren, I do things you wouldn't do. My youngest granddaughter is too thin, so whatever she wants to eat, I'm very happy. And if she brings into my kitchen a baloney sandwich from someplace I don't know, I put it on a paper plate. Should she want a little butter on a piece of pumpernickel, and if I should be so lucky, she also

wants to taste my breaded veal cutlet, out come the paper plates. But I promise you, God, only for a grandchild who's too thin, would I mix *milchig* and *fleishig*, and only on a paper plate."

She eats breaded
veal cutlet

She eats
baloney

Once in a while, I'd make brownies from scratch following the recipe on the box of Baker's unsweetened chocolate. But after melting, mixing, spilling, and licking, and after the brownies were baked, there'd only be enough for one brownie each for me, Tootsie, Ettie, and Mr. Goldberg.

Let me tell you something, don't believe what recipes say about how many portions or how many cookies. Recipes aren't written for Jews. If you're Jewish, whatever they say will feed half that number.

ETTIE NEVER WROTE DOWN any recipes, so once for Mother's Day I gave her a recipe box with index cards.

"Thank you very much but what am I supposed to do with this?" she asked.

"Ettie, you should write down how you make chicken soup, latkes, kugel, in case you get amnesia and can't remember."

"If I thought there were things I wouldn't remember, I'd get amnesia in a hurry," she said.

A few weeks later, I looked in the recipe box to see if she had written anything. Only one index card had writing. At the top of the card was written: *Make sure never to make Ida Bernstein's mock kishke recipe again.*

Below that was the recipe for Ida Bernstein's Mock Kishkes.

Whatever Ettie cooked, Mr. Goldberg ate as long as there was a bottle of Heinz ketchup on the table. He never worried about his big soup belly until one morning when Dr. Lewin, chief specialist of everything at Mount Sinai Hospital and a regular customer in the store, offered some free advice.

"Mr. Goldberg," Dr. Lewin began, "it's none of my business, but I think it would be wise for you to consider losing some weight."

Dr. Lewin was a brave man. Nobody else ever told Mr. Goldberg what to do.

When Mr. Goldberg told Ettie what the doctor had said, she said, "So I'll give you some free advice how to lose weight. Don't eat so much. Don't sit at the table and eat like it was your last meal. After a little of this and a little of that, say to yourself, 'Thank you very much, but I've had enough.' Also, have a little strawberry Jell-O or a little fruit cocktail for dessert instead of dessert. And it doesn't hurt to take a walk once in a while."

So Mr. Goldberg walked across the street to Duvanoy's, bought a Linzer tart, and then went upstairs for his afternoon nap.

Fruit Salad is good enough for Carmen Miranda!

Not Ettie

GRANDCHILDREN

ETTIE WASN'T LIKE ANY of my friends' grandmothers. She didn't bake cookies with Tootsie and me. She didn't knit us sweaters. She didn't sing us lullabies or songs from Broadway shows. Her arms weren't waiting for our hugs or to give us hugs. But Tootsie and I knew that she loved us.

Actually, I was sure that Ettie loved my sister best. Everybody loves the first child best. Even if the second child is adorable.

I wonder how different my life would have been if I had been the first child or first grandchild.

Tootsie had Veronica Lake wavy blonde hair with a dip over her left eye, eyes like light blue marbles, and long red fingernails that always matched her Revlon lipstick.

She had a voluptuous figure. Deliverymen whistled at her in the street and yelled out, "Hubba, hubba."

But her nose had a teeny, tiny bump she obsessed over, so she never felt pretty. Ettie was always telling her, "Don't worry about the size of your nose. The bigger it is, the better you can smell a flower."

Everybody else in the world thought Tootsie was just gorgeous.

Tootsie   **Veronica**

A nose is a
nose is a nose.
Gertrude Stein said that
and she was Jewish.

Besides the teeny, tiny bump in her nose, Tootsie had another problem. Me. Firstborn children seem to have that problem with the second child. "Why are you here?" they wonder. It never occurred to me at the time that being a first child came with its own set of problems. I had my own problems.

The five-year difference in our ages could have been a generation. Tootsie didn't have to buy dresses with Peter Pan collars and puffed sleeves.

Tootsie got whatever she wanted from Ettie, even a black dress with a sweetheart neckline.

Tootsie could go to the movies with a friend and didn't have to sit in the children's section.

Tootsie knew things I wanted to know. She knew how to raise one eyebrow, and she had kissed a boy.

Tootsie was old enough to work in the store in the summer. I wasn't. Ettie didn't know what to do with me. One customer suggested a summer camp in Smithfield, Maine, where I could take horseback riding lessons. Only three hundred dollars a week.

Great idea, Ettie said, and sent me to Cejwin Camp in Port Jervis, New York. Cejwin stood for Central Jewish Institute. It was kosher and cost three hundred dollars *for the whole summer.* Ettie sent me there every summer. "Thank you, God," she said, "for the big lake between the boys side and the girls side so I don't have to worry."

The first summer I was away, Ettie wrote me a letter I found many years later. It was stuck in the back of an old leather photo album.

Dear Maidele,

Are you eating? Stay away from the girl with lice and whatever you do don't go near her. She is probably a very nice girl but maybe she comes from Brooklyn and her mother doesn't clean the house so good. Don't tell her I said that. I will send you Drene Shampoo and a jar of Hellman's mayonnaise for the girl with bugs. Tell her to wash her hair with it and it will kill them. She should throw out the leftover mayonnaise—not eat it. I will send you two Goldenberg's Peanut Chews candy from the store and $1 but don't buy candy with the money. Have you made any friends yet who are from Manhattan? Make sure you are eating. They told me they give malted milk every day to the thin children. Let me know if you are getting malted milk every day because I am paying extra.

Your grandmother
from Madison Avenue

Dear Ma

Every time I compared myself to Tootsie, which was just about every day, I felt awful.

Every morning before school I complained to Ettie about the way I looked. My hair wasn't right, a pimple was starting, my nose and ears were growing, and worse.

"There is nothing wrong with how you look," she would say. "Even Rita Hayworth doesn't look so good in the morning.

"If you spent as much time thinking about what was going on on your insides instead of your outsides," Ettie would say, "you'd be a lot better off. Look at Emma Lazarus. She's no beauty and they made a big statue of her right in front of New York. Now that's a woman. She's Jewish, you know."

Dear God, maybe you know somebody who could make a movie about Emma Lazarus so everybody should know she's Jewish because even my granddaughter doesn't know.

To Ettie, not only did the Statue of Liberty have a poem on it by Emma Lazarus but it was of Emma Lazarus.

"You don't have to work so hard to get beautiful," Ettie said. "How many men would pay even a nickel to sit under a hot hair dryer for an hour every week just to get their hair like Tyrone Power?

"You think you can start out with a ten-cent ring from Woolworth's, pay somebody to shine it up at a beauty parlor, and people will think it's from Tiffany's?

"Only that guy with the big glasses can go into a telephone booth and come out looking like Superman."

Not even
Mr. Goldberg . . .

That same week, I found out I needed eyeglasses because I was nearsighted and braces on my teeth because they were buck.

"It's not the end of the world," Ettie told me. "There's already been a Jewish Miss America. Now we need a Jewish woman President—so go do your homework!"

Bess Meyerson, 1945

I was particularly jealous of Tootsie's bosom, but again Ettie told me not to worry. "Be grateful if your bosom looks like an ironing board. You'll always know that a man who falls in love with you loves you for your mind and not just because you have big titties. Who needs to schlep around an extra ten pounds anyway?"

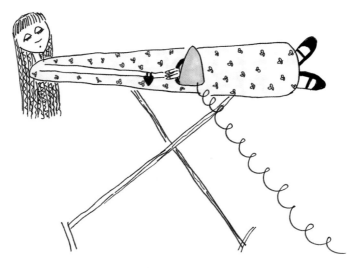

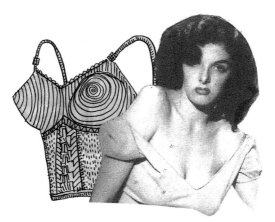

To Tootsie she said, "Be proud of your big bosom. A man doesn't want a woman whose front looks like her back."

Nobody knows the color of her eyes

While I worried about my bosom, Ettie worried about my bas mitzvah. She wanted Tootsie and me to have a Jewish education.

Everyone needs to believe in something. I have always been able to count on my faith in the power of Vaseline, chicken soup, and the Talmud.

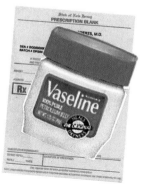

Works good all over

An Education

TOOTSIE WAS SEVENTEEN, past the conventional age to be bas mitzvahed. To me was going the honor.

Temple Emanu-El, the fanciest temple in New York, was on the corner of Fifth Avenue and 65th Street, a block away from the store.

Every day Rabbi Perilman, the head rabbi at Temple Emanuel, came into the store to buy the *Wall Street Journal*. Even though he was a Reform rabbi, he made a good impression on Mr. Goldberg. He always paid for the paper, unlike certain other customers who thought they were too important to pay the five cents.

Mr. Goldberg, however, would never step foot in Temple Emanu-El because the men didn't wear yarmulkes and the organ and choir made him feel like he was in a church. Mr. Goldberg went to Congregation Zichron Ephraim, the Orthodox temple on 67th Street between Lexington and Third avenues. He only went on the High Holidays. "Thank God that's over," he always said after the service.

Temple Emanu-El

A Reform temple is better than nothing.

Ettie always reminded Rabbi Perilman when the next Jewish holiday was, just in case.

One day Ettie whispered to Rabbi Perilman about her granddaughter, me, whose mother had died and whose father was no good and had disappeared, and that's how I became a scholarship student at Temple Emanu-El.

Sunday school at Temple Emanu-El meant I had to sit where Mrs. Burstein, the teacher, made me—between Rachel Kaplan and Sheri Rubinstein, who were best friends. Rachel's parents took her to Broadway shows and they sat in the sixth row, center. Sheri had a charm bracelet with charms that moved. You can imagine how I felt about Sundays.

To be bas mitzvahed from Temple Emanu-El, you had to be fourteen and they called it being confirmed. Ettie was planning a confirmation lunch for me at the Alrae Hotel on 64th Street. The manager of the restaurant in the hotel was a customer and, after Ettie talked to him about my situation, he said he would give her a good price if everybody came for an early lunch before his regulars.

Twenty people came and said *mazel tov*. My sister said my slip was showing. Ettie and Mr. Goldberg stood and didn't eat. The Alrae Hotel was *treif*. A waiter walked around with pigs in a blanket.

I should eat a pig? If I was starving, I'd stay starving.

Ettie bought me a Jewish star necklace as a confirmation
present. Two weeks later the clasp broke and I lost the
necklace.

When I told Ettie I had lost the necklace, I started
crying. *"Maideleh,"* she said, "don't cry about such a thing. It's
not your fault. Nothing is your fault. Save your tears. There'll
be time for tears when you're older."

If I wanted something from Ettie, the best way to get it was to let her think it had something to do with being Jewish. That's how I had my ears pierced. May 14, 1948, the day that Israel became a state, gave me a perfect opportunity.

Me: Ettie, I'm so happy Israel has become a state. So can you take me to get my ears pierced?

Ettie: So one thing has to do with the other, tell me? And who do you think you are anyway, a gypsy?

Me: Please?

Ettie: People will think you're Italian.

Me: Please, Please?

Ettie: People will think you just got off the boat.

Me: Ettie, please, all my friends are doing it.

Ettie: So all your friends are jumping in the lake, you're going to?

Me: Please!!!!!!

Ettie: You want a hole in your ear? Mr. Goldberg will say you have a hole in your head.

Me: Please, please, please, please! P L E A S E !!!!!!!!

Ettie: Putting holes in your ears will make you happy?

Me: Oh, yes, Ettie. For Israel. I'll never ask for another thing.

Ettie: *Bist meshugeh.* Okay. For Israel. Something to celebrate! Okay, we'll call the doctor. But don't let Mr. Goldberg ever know.

One time I had to write a paper in a high school English class about who I saw when I looked in the mirror. I asked Ettie, "So who do you see when you look in the mirror?"

"Who do you think I see," she said, "Lana Turner? I see a worried Jewish woman."

Ettie

Lana

Being Jewish was not the first thing I thought about when I looked in the mirror. What I saw was a teenage girl with glasses, braces on her teeth, Tangee on her lips, wearing her first bra, pink, 32AA.

I was growing older and changing. Ettie was growing old, but she couldn't change.

LOVE

WHEN I WAS FOURTEEN, I fell madly in love with
Mario, the delivery boy for Jesse's Kosher Butcher on Third
Avenue. He had his own bicycle. He delivered chickens to
Ettie every Friday morning.

But my romance never had a chance. I knew that if Ettie
ever found out I was madly in love with the butcher's delivery
boy who wore a cross around his neck, she'd give up chicken
and then kill herself.

Ettie's worst fear was that Tootsie or I would become
pregnant—by an Italian. Her third cousin Ida's daughter
Rachel eloped with an Italian boy named Tony and Ida never
heard from her daughter again.

Ettie once caught me kissing a date behind the stacks of
Sunday newspapers that were stored in the downstairs hallway.
She told my date that he should say good-bye and go
home to his mother. She told me: "Keep going the way you're
going, young lady, and you're going to get in big trouble
and ruin your life and have to leave the country like Ingrid
Bergman. Even worse, I'll tell Mr. Goldberg! I know about
these things. First comes holding hands, then the kiss, then a
lot of kisses and the touching, and before you know it, off come
the clothes. Then things happen you don't want to know."

INGRID, SHAME ON YOU

Big Scandal: Movie star Ingrid Bergman, married and a
mother, has affair with Italian director Rossellini, gets
pregnant, is denounced on the floor of the U.S. Senate,
and leaves country in shame.

"Oh, Ettie, weren't you ever young? Weren't you ever in love?" I asked her.

"What do you think," she answered. "I was always an old lady by the cash register? Just a while ago, I had a dream. Gregory Peck, a big movie star, calls me up. He wants I should go out with him Friday night."

"On Shabbat?" I say.

"But it's Gregory Peck and I always admire tall, dark, and handsome men like Robert Taylor, so I say yes.

"Friday night, he brings me a corsage and we go dancing. Then he asks me to go steady so I don't tell him about Mr. Goldberg.

"Then I woke up because I could smell the soup burning."

Gregory

So God, you made us dream so we'd have something else to laugh and cry about?

The only boy Tootsie ever dated was that boy from Westchester, even after they had each found out the other one had no money.

One day I got home from school early and surprised Tootsie and the boy on the couch. I saw her pulling down her shirt. But I could still tell her bra wasn't hooked.

The boy gave me a look. He didn't like me either.

Sex played no part in Ettie's life. She had three grown children. That was enough with under the covers. What she and Mr. Goldberg did in bed now was he snored and she worried.

But one night as I passed her bedroom door, I overheard her: "Oy, oy, oy. It hurts. I can't breathe. Oy, oy, oy. I'll have to wash and iron the sheets again."

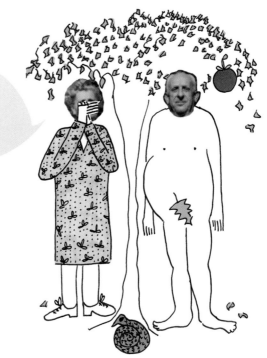

After she graduated from high school, Tootsie found a job as a gofer in the garment district. The job lasted only three days. Mr. Levy, the owner, had made a pass at her. She ran crying into the bathroom and stayed there until five o'clock.

She told Ettie what happened and that she was worried about what Mr. Levy would think. "Never worry what anybody thinks. Only worry what God thinks," Ettie told her.

"There is no excuse for a married Jew to make hanky-panky with someone who is not his wife, especially with a young girl who is my granddaughter.

"A Jew should not do such a thing to a young girl, to his wife, or to the Jewish people.

"A Jew doesn't have to be so special like Albert Einstein or Sophie Tucker, but after five thousand years of trouble, why look for trouble?

"You did the right thing," Ettie told her. "Levy did the wrong thing. Imagine, a married man. Imagine, a Jewish married man."

Ettie thought everyone should get married. Especially women. "But not to a Mr. Levy!"

She told Tootsie and me several times, "Marry a doctor. Everybody needs a doctor in the family, and with a doctor, you'll always know he's got a job because sooner or later everybody gets sick. And with a doctor, you're already a somebody. You're not just a Mr. and Mrs., you're a Dr. and Mrs. Plus, if you have a little chafing, a little wheezing, a little pain, you got somebody right there."

Don't waste your time on somebody who's not a doctor unless he's a dentist.

"Get them when you're young," Ettie advised us, "before somebody else gets them. Because if you aren't married by the time you are twenty-five, you will be an old maid. Nobody will ever want you, not even in a card game. You'll work as an assistant bookkeeper, live in a dark, tiny apartment, and have a cat that sheds on everything and ruins the vacuum cleaner. On Saturdays, you'll go to a movie with another old maid, then maybe splurge on a chocolate sundae with two scoops at Schrafft's."

"A man is different. If you're a man over thirty-nine and you're not married, it's a whole different ball game, a different kettle of fish, and horse of a different color. Nobody will ever call you an old butler. People will call you a bachelor, think you're a good catch, Cary Grant will play you in the movies, and unmarried women will make you noodle pudding."

You got to shop around to find a good fit

When Tootsie told Ettie that she and the boy from Westchester wanted to get married, Ettie wasn't as happy as Tootsie.

"You didn't look around enough," Ettie said, "A husband is like buying new shoes. You might see something you fall in love with right away, but if it's not a good fit, it will never make you happy."

"Well, at least he's Jewish," Tootsie said.

When Mr. Goldberg heard Tootsie's big announcement his response was: "Does he have a job, because I'm not hiring and I'm not supporting."

Despite Ettie's worries, something about The Announcement brought out a side of her I'd never known.

One afternoon when the store was empty, she started reminiscing. "Mr. Goldberg once told me he remembered the sound his footsteps made when he walked on the autumn leaves in the woods in Russia. I told him I remembered the crunching sound my boots made when I walked in the winter snow in Russia.

"I also remembered when I saw him for the first time in New Orleans and how I fell in love with him on the spot. But I didn't tell him that."

A NOTHER BEGINNING

TOOTSIE WANTED A WEDDING dress with a veil
and a train like the Junior League debutantes whose wedding
announcements and photographs by Bachrach she saw in the
Sunday *New York Times*.

Ettie was reluctant to spend the money for such a dress.
"You want a long, white dress with a train? Where are you
going to wear it again? To the butcher?"

Tootsie and the boy got married in the living room. She
wore a white wedding dress with a veil and a train.

It was the first time Ettie met the boy's mother. After the ceremony, Ettie took Tootsie aside and said, "I met the mother. So just make believe she's like a neighbor you hope you don't run into, but if you do, you say hello nicely and make believe she's a friend you're happy to see but you're in a hurry to go someplace else. God will forgive the lie."

Ettie handed her an envelope when Mr. Goldberg wasn't looking. Mr. Goldberg handed her an envelope when Ettie wasn't looking.

Nine months and a day later, Tootsie gave birth to a boy. "A great-grandchild, that's interest on the interest," Ettie said.

We had a bris. Mr. Goldberg held the baby with his eyes closed.

Ettie cried more than the baby. "At someone else's bris," she said, "I don't cry so many tears."

Tootsie didn't know whether to breast-feed or not. "Not even King Solomon could give you an answer," Ettie told her.

"Before there were bottles and formula, you didn't have a choice. But today, there is a modern way to do everything.

"Nobody should tell you what to do. Especially not your mother-in-law. Tell her to mind her own business—in a nice way."

"Some people think the only way is to breast-feed the baby. But some women don't have enough milk. Some women don't want to.

"Whichever way is okay by me. But no matter what you decide, whichever way you do, you should always hold your baby close."

RELATIVES

EVENTUALLY, MR. GOLDBERG'S father came north and eventually they started talking to each other.

After a few more years, Mr. Goldberg invited his father to the Passover seder.

I was supposed to call his father, my great-grandfather *Zayde*, but I never called him anything because I never spoke to him.

Zayde wore black from head to toe. I could see what he'd just eaten by looking at his beard. He spit when he talked. He'd run after me to tickle me and I'd run into the bathroom.

Dear God, You couldn't make Zayde should wear a red suit, carry jingle bells and go ho-ho-ho once in a while, so my granddaughter shouldn't be scared?

Three sisters, Minnie, Sarah, and Rose were cousins of Mr. Goldberg. They never married and lived from hand to mouth in Brooklyn. Sometimes they came into the store.

Minnie was an elementary school teacher, Sarah was a social worker, and Rose cooked and cleaned for her sisters, listened to Woody Guthrie records, and wrote letters to Henry Wallace, the 1948 Progressive candidate for president of the United States, endorsed by the U.S. Communist Party.

On Saturdays, the sisters marched in protest. On Sundays, the sisters distributed flyers. Evenings, the sisters knitted sweaters for the oppressed. They could sing "The International," the anthem of world socialism, in harmony.

"Let me tell you about three other sisters," Ettie said. "Patty, LaVerne, and Maxene—the Andrews sisters. They go around singing "Bei Mir Bist du Schon" and they aren't even Jewish. But from that song, they make a fortune and live in sunny California.

"Sometimes life is all about the song you sing."

Maxene   Patty   LaVerne

Mr. Goldberg called his cousins the Pinko Sisters. Thanks to Ettie, they never left the store empty handed.

Ettie would always say, "Take a magazine, a piece of candy. Maybe you want a Tootsie Roll? Some Chiclets? Mason Dots? Necco Wafers? Maybe you'll be lucky and find a Necco with a lot of chocolate wafers. Don't be shy. You need some Waterman's blue-black ink? Don't worry, I'll deal with Mr. Goldberg."

Almost every Jewish family had an unmarried aunt. In ours, Aunt Babbie occupied that unenviable position. I loved it when she came to visit. She always brought a shiny box of Fanny Farmer lollipops.

Instead of marriage, Babbie choose a career. She worked as head bookkeeper for the Elite Dress Company. She excelled at her job. Her numbers were always balanced. Her profit and loss statements were accurate to the penny. However, her reconciliation of pluses and minuses did not translate into her choice or appraisals of men.

A bright tie on a charming shoulder-pad salesman blinded her to the fact that Irving Grossman was about to be jailed for embezzlement.

Lou Stein, who always wore a vest, opened the door for her, and took her dancing at Roseland, obscured the small detail that he'd been married for seventeen years and had two teenage sons.

Eventually, Babbie abandoned the garment industry and migrated to Florida.

Unlike the birds, though, she never came back.

Holidays

THE STORE WAS OPEN seven days a week including holidays, with one exception.

The one day a year the store was closed was Yom Kippur.

There was always a contest of wills between Ettie and Mr. Goldberg, and it was never more apparent than on a Jewish holiday.

One particular Passover, we sat down for the seder when Mr. Goldberg stood up and announced "Before we will begin the seder, we will sing 'Hatikvah.'"

"'Hatikvah?'" Ettie countered, "We are Americans. We should sing 'The Star Spangled Banner.'"

Mr. Goldberg: We will sing "Hatikvah"!

Ettie: Mr. Goldberg, you're an American.

Mr. Goldberg: "Hatikvah"!

Ettie: "The Star Spangled Banner"!

Mr. Goldberg: So all of a sudden you're Mrs. George Washington? Enough already. The people who want to sing "Hatikvah" should go by my side of the table. The people who want to sing the other song should go by her side of the table.

Nobody moved. Mr. Goldberg and Ettie both stood at opposite ends of the Passover table. Mr. Goldberg sang "Hatikvah" loud. Ettie sang "The Star Spangled Banner" louder.

The seder had begun.

Ettie never looked forward to Passover even if just Zayde and the Pinko sisters came.

"It isn't the planning," she'd say.

"It isn't about cleaning the house."

"It isn't about finding enough chairs or enough glasses."

"It isn't about the shopping."

"It isn't even about the cooking."

"It's about how to keep everything hot when you've only got a small oven."

Every Passover, Mr. Goldberg complained that the brisket was too dry and there wasn't enough of it, the chicken didn't have enough dark meat, the chicken soup was too salty, the matzah balls weren't fluffy enough, the chicken liver gave him heartburn, and next year, *he'd* make the *charosis* so it would come out right.

So you listening, God? Boils, blood, lice, wild beasts, pestilence, hail, locusts, darkness, slaying the firstborn—that's nothing compared to what I go through in a week with Mr. Goldberg.

One year, Ettie wanted to buy a new hat for
Rosh Hashanah. "Not like I don't have a hat, but Mrs.
Schneiderman who sits next to me at the temple, her son
is already a doctor, might think I have only one hat. She has
a hat with a big feather. I want a hat with a bigger feather."

So Ettie decided to go to Klein's on 14th Street and she
asked me to go with her. Klein's was known for its bargains
and Ettie was always trying to save money. Still, we took a
taxi down to 14th Street.

Once we got to Klein's, we took the escalator up to the third floor. Ettie didn't go on elevators.

Why ride up and down in a closet? On the escalator, in case there's a fire, I can get off in a hurry.

Ettie avoided saleswomen. "Saleswomen get commissions on what they sell," she told me by way of instruction, "so they try to sell me a lot of expensive *shmattes*. I have nothing against a woman should make a living, but not from me."

As soon as we reached the floor where they sold ladies' hats, a saleswoman asked Ettie if she needed any help. "No, thank you," Ettie said. "I'm just looking. I'm not buying anything today. Thank you very much but no thank you. I'm just looking and I don't even know what I'm looking for. But by the way, should you know where the black hats with big feathers are, you might point me in that direction."

We walked to the corner section where they had ladies' hats. Ettie picked up a hat, looked at the tag, and said, "Who can afford this? Mrs. Rockefeller, maybe. Maybe I should call Mr. Goldberg's cousin Morris. His son sells mattresses in the garment district. Maybe he could get me with a big feather wholesale?"

I reminded Ettie that Mr. Goldberg and Morris hadn't spoken in years.

"Maybe it's about time," she answered.

Purim was no big *megillah* for Ettie. "Any Jewish holiday when you don't you cry or starve isn't worth fussing over," she told me.

Every December, the store was decked out with Christmas ornaments and boxes and boxes of Christmas cards. One small shelf in the back of the store held about six Chanukah cards.

The spelling of *Chanukah* was a continuous battle between Ettie and Mr. Goldberg for they needed a small sign. Ettie spelled it Hanuka. Mr.Goldberg spelled it Chanukah.

One day, Mr. Goldberg insisted. "I'm right," he said. "It's written Challah, not hallah, so, once again, I am right."

Ettie believed in tradition. Every Hanuka she said the same things:

1. Don't eat the chocolate Hanuka gelt all at once, you'll get constipated.
2. Eat the latkes while they're hot, but don't eat too many, you'll get diarrhea.
3. Not so much sugar, your teeth will fall out.
4. Eat, eat. There are children starving in Europe.

Every time Ettie heard Bing Crosby sing "White Christmas" on the radio, she muttered, "Irving Berlin, a Jew, wrote that song. So what would have been so terrible if he'd dreamed about a white Hanuka, instead?"

Let me tell you something, Bing Crosby is no Al Jolson.

Sukkot Ettie completely ignored.

Thank you, God, for a
holiday so beautiful, but on Madison
Avenue nobody puts up a sukkah. *Lulav*, they don't
sell in Gristede's. Times have changed. I don't
worry about the Cossacks anymore, I worry
about shoplifters.

Cossacks

But even if her feet hurt, her head hurt, or her heart hurt, even if she was too tired to move, even if it was too hot, too cold, too windy, too snowy, even if it got dark too early or too late, Ettie always lit the *Shabbos* candles.

A WAY OF LIFE ENDS.
A NEW ONE BEGINS.

ETTIE WAS ALWAYS a little sad on a Jewish holiday. On one hand, she wanted to be observant. On the other hand, the holidays didn't fit in with life on Madison Avenue. "How can we close the store for Shabbos, for Tish'a B'Av, for Simchat Torah, for Rosh Hashanah? We'll lose customers. They'll go to 59th Street for their newspapers."

"Who knows what to do anymore?

"Who knows what's important anymore?

"Who even knows who anybody is anymore," she sighed.

"Nobody knows that Hedy Lamarr is really Jewish." On and on she'd go. Her list was endless. Anybody she admired was in one way or another Jewish.

"And Cary Grant is part Jewish, but I don't know which part. Lauren Bacall is Jewish and married Humphrey Bogart who also has a Jewish part. Winston Churchill and Mae West have Jewish mothers. Groucho Marx and his brothers are all Jewish. The Ritz brothers, Jewish, but Jews shouldn't hit each other on the head. Jacob Javits, the senator in Washington, is Jewish, so I don't think he's really a Republican."

"Three more things, you should always remember:

"Number 1: Rich or poor, it's good to have money.

"Number 2: You better eat something while you're waiting for a free lunch.

"Number 3: Nobody owes you anything unless you lend them money and it should be in writing on a piece of paper with a lot of copies and a lawyer who puts a seal on it with a notary. And try to use a Jewish lawyer.

"You know why there are so many Jewish lawyers? It's in our history to argue. Do you know a Jew who doesn't have an opinion?

"Adam and Eve, Cain and Abel, Joseph and his brothers—it's in our history not to get along.

"Fight with guns? We like to fight with words.

"The men sit and study the Talmud and they discuss, they debate, they argue, their faces turn red, they start to shake, and worse things happen."

God, how come every Jew is putting in his two cents, especially if nobody asked him?

IN THIS LIFE, YOU have to be prepared," Ettie advised, and she always was.

Whenever she left the store she carried with her a black pocketbook with a gold clasp that made a noise when she closed it. It was her Handbag for Emergencies.

No matter when I looked in it, I always found the same things:

Peppermint Life Savers
A white cotton handkerchief with
    embroidered flowers
A small mirror in a felt case
A compact with a powder puff and powder (never used)
Ten shiny pennies (for the *kinder* to play with) and a dollar
    in change in a red leather change purse
A silver pillbox with four aspirins inside
A plastic rain bonnet in a plastic holder
A safety pin
A small sewing kit from the Saxony Hotel in Miami Beach
A Band-Aid
A five-dollar bill rolled up and stuffed into the pinky of a
    pair of short black cotton gloves
    The telephone number of Mr. Max
    Finklestein, a lawyer: TRafalga 8-9224.

You never know when you might get a splinter.

ENDINGS

FINALLY, HIGH SCHOOL was over for me. What would
I do? What were my choices?

"Let me give you some good advice," Ettie said. "Smart
people are smart because they make smart choices. There are
some things maybe you want to do, but you don't do them
good. It wouldn't be smart to choose them to make a living.

"Not everybody can do everything. Maybe I want to be
like Gypsy Rose Lee. Let me tell you, Gypsy Rose Lee doesn't
have to worry I'm going to take her job. But I bet Gypsy Rose
Lee can't make a breaded veal cutlet
as good as me. Some things you
can do. Some things you never
can do."

A smart person
knows what he can't do, but a
smart aleck thinks he can
do everything.

"I'm not telling you what to do," Ettie said, "but you should go to college. Today everybody needs to go. In college is where you get smart and after you get smart, you get rich. And in college is where you'll find a husband.

"Go to Boston. They have schools there for doctors and lawyers. Go look for one."

So I left my life on Madison Avenue and I started a new life as a college freshman in Boston.

Ettie, Mr. Goldberg, the store, and my "situation," as Ettie would say, disappeared before the train even got to Back Bay.

Ettie was in her seventies by the time I left for Boston. She had never lied about her age.

"A spring chicken I'm not," she often said, "but I remember what it's like to be young.

"When you're young, you think you'll always be young. You can't imagine that the day will come when you'll be happy just to have a nice hot glass of tea with lemon, a good bowel movement, a glass to put your teeth in, and praise God because you slept through the night and woke up in the morning without a pain."

When Ettie was in her nineties, she lay dying on the green couch in the living room. I saw Mr. Goldberg kneel down next to her and take her hand. With tears in his eyes, he said, "You know, Mrs. Goldberg, I could have done a lot worse."

Let me tell you something, if you're lucky, you'll get old.

Epilogue

Ettie's death wasn't a great loss to the world, but it was to me. Many years had passed since I had lived at 743 Madison Avenue. I was busy with children of my own. Often I found myself saying to them the same words Ettie had said to me. More time passed and I had grandchildren. I remember Ettie saying there were things I wouldn't understand until I became a grandmother.

How right she was.

This book is dedicated to Ettie
by her seventy-five-year-old granddaughter

I lene Beckerman's beloved and bestselling book has been adapted for the stage by Nora and Delia Ephron. The star-studded Off-Broadway show is receiving rave reviews, as did the book:

"Illuminates the experience of an entire generation of women . . . This small gem of a book is worthy of a Tiffany box." —*The New York Times Book Review*

"Never has the love of beautiful clothes seemed less frivolous." —*The New Yorker*

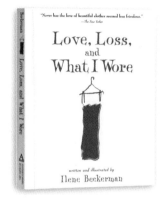

ISBN 978-1-56512-475-2

I nspired by a school reunion, Beckerman addresses what really matters in life.

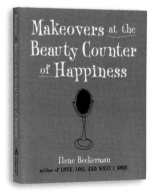

"[An] eloquent blend of memoir and down-to-earth advice . . . makes these lessons not only worth learning, but irresistible as well." —*The Common Reader*

"Cuts to the heart of the female experience." —*Chicago Tribune*

ISBN 978-1-56512-374-8

T he highs and lows of a relationship with an adult daughter
are revealed in this poignant and candid story.

"Pithy wit and cute drawings sketch the
happy tears, bittersweet memories and flares
of anxiety that a daughter's wedding elicits."
—*The Dallas Morning News*

"This is no mere humor book. Amid the drolleries
are the poignant reflections of a mother."
—Beliefnet.com

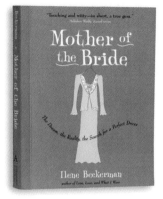

ISBN 978-1-56512-476-9

L ooking for love is never easy, and it's never what you expect.
This eloquent book is a reminder of how true that is.

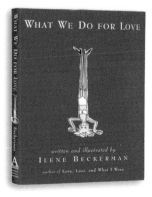

"This savory little truffle turns out to be
surprisingly poignant, laced with the bitter, the
rueful, and the sweet." —*Good Housekeeping*

"Few contemporary authors capture the poignancy
of romantic feeling in the spare, subtle way
Ilene Beckerman does."
—*USA Today*

ISBN 978-1-56512-180-5